Facts About the Pelican

By Lisa Strattin

© 2019 Lisa Strattin

Facts for Kids Picture Books by Lisa Strattin

Little Blue Penguin, Vol 92

Chipmunk, Vol 5

Frilled Lizard, Vol 39

Blue and Gold Macaw, Vol 13

Poison Dart Frogs, Vol 50

Blue Tarantula, Vol 115

African Elephants, Vol 8

Amur Leopard, Vol 89

Sabre Tooth Tiger, Vol 167

Baboon, Vol 174

Sign Up for New Release Emails Here

http://LisaStrattin.com/subscribe-here

Monthly Surprise Box

http://KidCraftsByLisa.com

Contents

INTRODUCTION

The pelican is a large bird that is well-known for the pouch that is in its beak which the pelican uses to scoop fish out if the water. The pelican is found in the countryside worldwide, dwelling near water and densely populated fishing areas.

The brown sea pelican is one of the largest species of pelican with male pelicans often leaving the flock to hunt alone at sea. The brown pelican is particularly remarkable for its ability to swoop down to the ocean surface from enormous heights to catch fish.

CHARACTERISTICS

There are eight different species of pelican found on every continent in the world with the exception of the Antarctic. Pelicans tend to prefer the more temperate and warmer climates to the colder ones, and pelicans are therefore most commonly found closer to the Equator.

APPEARANCE

The pelican is generally an enormous bird with some species gaining a wingspan of well over 9 feet. Other species of pelican are much smaller but these smaller species of pelican tend to live on land rather than spending their lives at sea.

LIFE STAGES

During the breeding season, pelicans nest in colonies and breeding usually begins with a group of male pelicans chasing a single female pelican. The pelican courtship can occur on land, in the air or on water. The male pelican collects materials to build the nest which the female pelican then uses to build a nest either on the ground or in a tree depending on the pelican species.

The female pelican lays an average clutch size of 2 to 6 eggs which both the female pelican and the male pelican help incubate. After an period of around a month, the pelican chicks hatch out of their eggs but many times, only one or two chicks will survive out of the clutch.

The female pelican feeds her young until they are around 3 months old, although baby pelicans are usually able to walk and swim when they are about 2 months old.

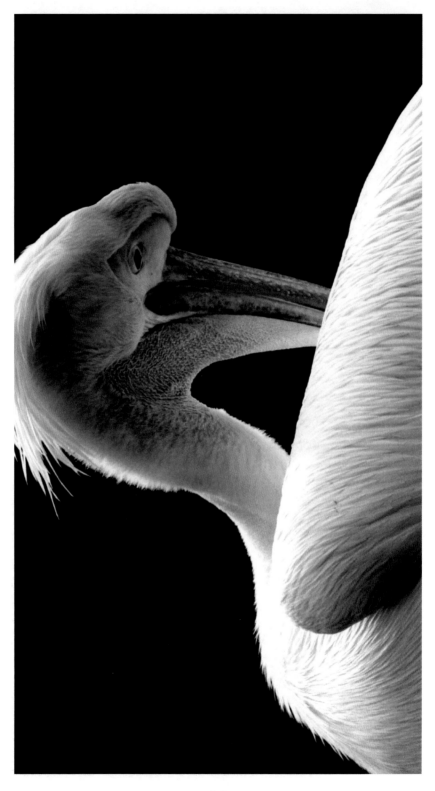

LIFE SPAN

Pelicans have been recorded to live for 16 to 23 years.

SIZE

Pelicans are usually between 3.5 to 6 feet tall with a wingspan of 6 to 10 feet. They can weigh between 6 to 34 pounds. They really are a very large bird!

HABITAT

Pelicans inhabit areas around the world, usually living in large flocks of more than 100 birds. They rest and nest together in these flock communities, but often hunt and feed alone. The only exception to this is when the female pelican is feeding her chicks. The chicks are known to gather together in small groups within the communal nesting site of their parents.

DIET

Despite the fact that they are omnivorous, pelicans mostly feed on fish, crustaceans such as prawns and crabs, small species of turtles and squids. The pelican uses the beak pouch to scoop a mouth-full of water up and then strains the water out of its beak leaving the fish and other food in the pouch for the pelican to eat.

FRIENDS AND ENEMIES

Due to their generally large size, pelicans have only a few predators in their natural environment. Wild dogs, like the coyotes, are one of the main predators of the pelican along with cats and humans who hunt the pelican for their meat and feathers.

Their main friends are the other pelicans in their flock, although they commonly get along with other birds in the areas where they live.

SUITABILITY AS PETS

A pelican would not be a great choice for a pet. They are just too big! But they are entertaining to watch when you are visiting a beach where they live.

COLOR ME

COLOR ME

COLOR ME

COLOR ME

COLOR ME

Please leave me a review here:

http://lisastrattin.com/Review-Vol-191

For more Kindle Downloads Visit Lisa Strattin Author Page on Amazon Author Central

http://amazon.com/author/lisastrattin

To see upcoming titles, visit my website at LisaStrattin.com– all books available on kindle!

http://lisastrattin.com

PLUSH PELICAN TOY

You can get one by copying and pasting this link into your browser:

http://lisastrattin.com/PelicanPlush

MONTHLY SURPRISE BOX

Get yours by copying and pasting this link into your browser

http://KidCraftsByLisa.com

Made in the USA
Columbia, SC
13 December 2021